ELIZABETH I
and Tudor England

by Miriam Greenblatt

BENCHMARK BOOKS

MARSHALL CAVENDISH
NEW YORK

ACKNOWLEDGMENT

With thanks to Dr. Ethan H. Shagan, Assistant Professor of History
at Northwestern University, Evanston, Illinois,
for his expert reading of the manuscript.

Benchmark Books
Marshall Cavendish Corporation
99 White Plains Road
Tarrytown, New York 10591-9001
Website: www.marshallcavendish.com

Copyright © 2002 by Miriam Greenblatt

Library of Congress Cataloging-in-Publication Data
Greenblatt, Miriam.
Elizabeth I and Tudor England / by Miriam Greenblatt.
p. cm. — (Rulers and their times)
Includes bibliographical references (p.) and index.
Summary: Examines the reign of Elizabeth I, including information about her personal life and accomplishments and everyday life in Tudor England, plus contemporary writings which characterize the Elizabethan Age.
ISBN 0-7614-1028-7 (lib. bdg.)
1. Elizabeth I, Queen of England, 1533–1603—Juvenile literature. 2. Great Britain—History—Elizabeth, 1558–1603—Juvenile literature. 3. Great Britain—History—Tudors, 1485–1603—Juvenile literature. 4. Queens—Great Britain—Biography—Juvenile literature. [1. Elizabeth I, Queen of England, 1533–1603. 2. Kings, queens, rulers, etc. 3. Great Britain—History—Elizabeth, 1558–1603. 4. Great Britain—Social life and customs—16th century.] I. Title. II. Series.
DA355 .G47   2001   942.05′5′092—dc21   00-057209

Printed in Hong Kong
1 3 5 6 4 2

Photo Research by Linda Sykes Photo Research, Hilton Head SC
Photo Credits are on page 88

Permission has been granted to use extended quotations from the following copyrighted works:

"An Old Man's Lesson" by Nicholas Breton, in *Elizabethan Women*, ed. Gamaliel Bradford. Copyright © 1936, renewed 1964 by Sara Bradford Ross. Reprinted by permission of Houghton Mifflin Company. All rights reserved.

"A New Ballad of the Life and Deaths of Three Witches Arraigned and Executed at Chelmsford 5 July 1589," in *Witchcraft Papers*, ed. Peter Haining. London: Robert Hale & Co., 1974. Reprinted by permission of Peter Haining.

"The Twelve Moneths and Christmas Day" in *Fantastickes* by Nicholas Breton, ed. Bruce Rogers. New York: Clarke & Way, 1951.

Diary of Lady Margaret Hoby, 1599–1605, ed. Dorothy M. Meads. New York: Houghton Mifflin Company, 1930.

A translated passage from Pena, Pierre, and Matthias de l'Obel, "Stirpium Adversaria Nova" (London, 1570–1771). Published in *Tobacco: Its History Illustrated by the Books, Manuscripts and Engravings in the Library of George Arents Jr.* by Jerome E. Brooks, Volume One 1507–1615. New York: The Rosenbach Company, 1937, p. 239–240. Reprinted by permission of the Arents Collection, New York Public Library.

Contents

A New Age

England in the time of Elizabeth I (1533–1603) was a land on the verge of becoming a nation. It was in the final stage of changing from a collection of estates, each ruled by a noble, into a country to which its people gave "a passionate loyalty." It was shifting its official religion from Catholicism to Protestantism. Where once most English subjects had been farmers, now more and more were becoming merchants. Involved in international trade, they began to send out ships to explore and colonize other parts of the world. Even the English language was developing a remarkable richness under the leadership of such writers as William Shakespeare.

Other rulers in history have had periods named after them. Yet the Elizabethan Age is better known than most, largely because of the personality of its great queen. In this book, you will learn about the life and accomplishments of this remarkable woman. You will see how she met the religious, personal, and political challenges that confronted her during her long reign. You will see how the English people lived and worked. And you will read diaries, poems, ballads, and other accounts in which Elizabethans tell us about themselves in their own words.

Most portraits of Elizabeth look alike. They emphasize the details of her clothing and jewelry, and contain symbols of purity, like the white ermine edging of her gown.

PART ONE

"She Certai

Elizabeth's court was not only a center of government. It was also a center of entertainment, where banquets, balls, and tournaments were common.

A Difficult and Dangerous Youth

Elizabeth Tudor was born September 7, 1533. She was a pretty little thing, with reddish gold hair and dark eyes. Church bells rang out in celebration, and people lit bonfires and drank toasts in her honor. Elizabeth's father, however, was bitterly disappointed. Henry VIII already had a daughter, the princess Mary. What he wanted was a male heir to the throne.

Henry had been trying to divorce his first wife, Catherine (Mary's mother), for some time because she had not borne him a son. When the pope refused to annul, or cancel, their marriage, Henry broke with the Roman Catholic Church and declared himself "head of the English Church, subject only to God."

Henry's action angered Catholics both at home and abroad. So to strengthen his political position, he gave Protestants new power in the English church and in the English government. This set England on the road to becoming a Protestant rather than a Catholic country. It also meant that money from the English church would no longer go to Rome but would stay in England. Several years later, in fact, Henry disbanded the Catholic monasteries and took their lands and treasure for himself and his political allies. In the meantime he divorced Catherine and married Anne Boleyn, Elizabeth's mother.

Henry VIII spent six years trying to persuade his first wife to give him a divorce so that he could marry Anne Boleyn, pictured above. A flirtatious beauty with large black eyes and a long neck, Anne was also very intelligent and well educated.

The pope, whose authority in Europe had been severely damaged by the king's actions, retaliated by excommunicating Henry. In the Church's eyes, he was no longer king and his subjects were not obliged to obey him.

Anne became pregnant two more times after giving birth to Elizabeth, but neither baby (both of whom were apparently boys) lived. So history more or less repeated itself. Determined to have a male heir, Henry ordered Anne beheaded on a charge of high treason and took a third wife, Jane Seymour. This time the king got what he wanted. In 1537, when Elizabeth was four years old, Jane gave birth to a son, named Edward.

With Edward's birth, Elizabeth's life turned topsy-turvy. When she had been born, Henry had named her heir to the throne in place of her half sister, Mary. Elizabeth had received the title of Princess of Wales, a palace and servants of her own, and the right to be carried from place to place in a velvet litter. Now her half brother, Edward, was named heir to the throne, her royal title was taken away, and her household reduced to a mere thirty persons, all of them "ancient and sad."

Despite this change, Elizabeth received an excellent education. She was a natural student. She began learning Latin when she was about five years old and soon added Flemish, French, Greek, Italian, Spanish, and even a little Welsh to her collection of languages. She loved history and is said to have studied it for three hours every day. She took lessons in architecture, astronomy, geography, and mathematics. Lighter subjects included dancing, etiquette, horseback riding, and sewing.

In 1547 Henry VIII died, and Edward VI became king of England. Unfortunately, the young boy was easily manipulated by ambitious politicians. Among the results was a scandal involving Elizabeth and Thomas Seymour, one of Edward's uncles. Suspected of having an affair with Seymour, the fifteen-year-old Elizabeth declared that she had nothing to hide and presented herself at court as "a virtuous maid" dressed in simple clothes of black and white. Her behavior quickly won her the good opinion of the English people. As one historian comments, "Already she understood how vital were appearances. For the rest of her life, she would woo the English, knowing that their love and respect would be her shield against danger."

Thomas Seymour was beheaded, but Elizabeth was safe. A few

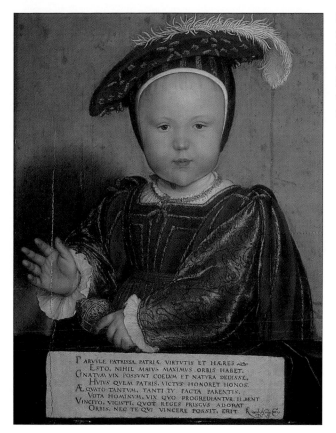

Edward VI inherited the throne of England when he was just nine years old. He died at the age of fifteen from tuberculosis, which doctors apparently treated with arsenic.

years later, in 1553, Edward VI died, and after some political maneuvering, Elizabeth's half sister, Mary, ascended the throne. Religious strife broke out almost at once.

During Edward's reign, Protestantism had grown stronger among the English. Mary, a fervent Catholic, was determined to lead her subjects "back to the true Church." Apparently she thought it would be easy. She did not realize that nobles who had received land and money when the monasteries were disbanded would be reluctant to give them back. Nor did she realize that most English people felt it would be unpatriotic for them to be controlled by a foreign pope.

At the same time, Protestant extremists believed that not enough religious reforms had been made. They began destroying church altars and attacking priests. A month after Mary became queen, Londoners were rioting in the streets over whether a Latin or an English prayer book should be used in church services.

Elizabeth, like her mother and her tutors, was a Protestant. This put her in a difficult position. On the one hand, she could not take a stand against the queen by supporting Mary's Protestant opponents. On the other hand, she could not become a Catholic, as Mary wanted her to. If she did, it would have meant acknowledging that her parents' marriage was illegal and that she herself was a bastard without any right to the throne.

Matters became even more difficult when Mary—against the advice of Parliament—decided to marry the Catholic Prince Philip, heir to the throne of Spain. The idea of being ruled by a foreign king horrified the English, and several nobles (including some Catholics) organized a conspiracy against the queen. The plot was discovered, and the rebels were hanged. A few days later, Mary ordered the twenty-year-old Elizabeth imprisoned in the Tower of London.

Elizabeth spent two miserable months in prison. She suffered from migraine headaches and a kidney infection. She expected that each day would be her last and that she would be beheaded as her mother had been. Finally, however, after a thorough investigation showed that she had not known about the rebellion against Mary, she was allowed to leave the Tower for house arrest in a country manor.

Mary and Philip were married in July 1554. At Philip's urging, the queen recalled Elizabeth to court. She then insisted that

Philip arrived in England accompanied by some nine thousand nobles and servants. He was reluctant to wed Mary, who was eleven years his senior, but felt it was his duty to keep England allied with Spain.

Elizabeth marry one of Philip's allies, the duke of Savoy. Elizabeth, however, refused to wed a foreigner. She would rather die, she said. She fell ill again, and Mary stopped pressuring her half sister.

Mary did not, however, stop trying to make her subjects Catholic. In February 1555 her government began burning Protestants at the stake in the village of Smithfield, just outside London. About three hundred men and women died in the flames. Their deaths became known as "the Smithfield Fires," and the queen soon became known as "Bloody Mary."

Making matters worse was the fact that Philip dragged England into a war with Spain against France. The war went badly for the English, who lost the city of Calais, which they had held for

Mary Tudor had a raspy voice and a melancholy disposition. The longer she ruled, the grimmer she became.

more than two hundred years. The loss damaged Mary's popularity still further.

At last, on November 17, 1558, Mary Tudor died, probably from cancer. Twenty-five-year-old Elizabeth was queen of England.

Taking Charge

Elizabeth's first act was to form a loyal government. As her secretary of state, she chose William Cecil, later Lord Burghley, a discreet and able individual who would serve her for the next forty years. She dismissed most members of Mary's privy council and replaced them with a broad range of advisers, including lawyers and businessmen as well as nobles.

Elizabeth's second act was to hold a brilliant and lavish coronation procession. New clothes were ordered for members of the royal household. The holes in London's streets were filled and fresh gravel scattered on top. Elizabeth rode in a litter covered with gold brocade and lined with white satin. Footmen dressed in crimson velvet marched on either side. The litter was preceded by church officials and foreign ambassadors, and was followed by hundreds of courtiers on horseback. Every now and then, the procession stopped to watch a pageant or listen to a welcoming speech. People thrust flowers at their new monarch, while church bells pealed and bonfires blazed.

Elizabeth smiled and waved. She was gracious to everyone who approached her, frequently crying out, "God thank you all." She was developing her image of Good Queen Bess, the ruler who was devoted to her subjects and courted their good opinion. She was also developing her image of Gloriana, the goddess around whom England revolved.

Elizabeth, resplendent in white and gold and satin and lace, makes one of her frequent public outings. This time she is on her way to a wedding.

Throughout her reign, Elizabeth continued to develop both images. Each summer, she made what was known as a progress from London to one or more of her courtiers' estates. Along the way she carefully observed the condition of the countryside and the mood of the people. "Everywhere she went, she told her subjects how she loved them and reminded them often that they loved her." She was kind to ordinary people. When fireworks burned down a commoner's house, she had a new one built for him. When the women in a village prepared a banquet for her, she ate the food without having it tasted first for poison, thus showing the women her complete trust.

Elizabeth's court dazzled people with its splendor. It was the center of the nation's power and wealth. Everyone with a spark of ambition came there to seek their fortunes—playwrights, musicians, young men in search of government positions, and beautiful women looking for rich husbands. People competed strenuously for the queen's attention. They often spent all they had on elegant clothes. Of course they flattered Elizabeth, praising her courage, her wisdom, and especially her beauty. They showered her with gifts, usually items for her wardrobe, such as rich fabrics and huge colored jewels. Yet they also made fun of her behind her back. It was difficult for them to accept being ruled by an unmarried woman.

A Religious Compromise

The most immediate difficulty that confronted Elizabeth after her coronation was a religious one. For twenty-five years, the country had been pulled one way by Catholics, another way by Protestants. What form would England's religion take under its new ruler?

Elizabeth's answer to the question was typical of how she handled problems throughout her reign. Instead of coming down on one side or the other, she tried to be practical and to steer a middle course between extremes.

Under the terms of the Religious Settlement of 1559, there was only one official church, the Church of England. But rather than calling herself its supreme head as Henry VIII had done, Elizabeth was content with the title of supreme governor. That meant leaving the final decision on matters of faith up to the church hierarchy. At the same time, all church officials were required to swear absolute loyalty to the queen. So were all government officials, teachers, and other persons of authority. Under Elizabeth, religion and nationality were almost the same.

The church kept its altars, tapestries, crucifixes, and candles. On the other hand, priests were now allowed to marry. However, they continued to wear clerical robes. The Book of Common Prayer

The man in the right foreground of this painting is Robert Cecil, son of William Cecil. Like his father, Robert Cecil served as secretary of state. Elizabeth's advisers were paid low wages, but they received gifts of land, jewels, and the exclusive rights to sell certain goods, such as spices, raisins, or wine.

written under Edward VI was reissued, but language designed to satisfy Catholics was added.

Adults were required to attend church services in their local parish on Sundays and holy days. If they failed to do so, they were fined. Services, which were now conducted in English rather than Latin, included the singing of hymns by the parishioners, readings from the Old and New Testaments, and, especially, a sermon, which sometimes lasted as long as three hours. The government issued books of approved sermons that emphasized "religious conformity and political obedience." A priest needed a special license if he wanted to preach a sermon that he himself had written. Children were expected to learn the Ten Commandments, the Articles of Belief, the Lord's Prayer, and the catechism by heart.

At the same time, Elizabeth was not overly concerned about people's religious beliefs or the practices they followed in private. What mattered to her was outward conformity. Accordingly, Bible reading in homes became common. People discussed the meaning of religion among themselves. And both Catholics and radical Protestants (such as the Puritans) were usually tolerated throughout Elizabeth's reign except if they challenged her political position.

The Question of Marriage

The next difficulty that confronted Elizabeth was a more personal one. Parliament and the country alike wanted her to marry. After all, they said, she was only a woman, and no matter how intelligent and well educated, she needed the help of a man in order to govern. That was nature's law and the law of God. There was another reason for urging the queen to marry. Who would succeed her if she did not produce an heir?

The first suitor to present himself was Mary's widower, King Philip of Spain. But he would agree to the marriage only if Elizabeth became a Catholic. Since that was out of the question, the matter was dropped.

Other suitors followed, including the king of Sweden, the archduke of Austria, and a French prince. Elizabeth made each of them in turn think that a marital alliance between their country and England was near at hand. That enabled her to keep other countries off balance. But in each case, Elizabeth eventually rejected her suitor. She realized that the English people would not be happy with a foreign king. Besides, in her eyes she already had a husband, namely, England. Once, when addressing Parliament, she even took her coronation ring from her finger and held it up, saying, "Behold . . . The Pledge of this my

Wedlock and Marriage with my Kingdom."

There was another reason for the queen's reluctance to wed. According to most scholars, she was in love with Robert Dudley, later the earl of Leicester. The two had much in common. They had played together as children. They had had the same tutor. They had both been imprisoned at the same time in the Tower of London. They were both full of energy and loved to ride, hunt, and dance the night away. Nevertheless, even after Dudley's wife broke her neck in a fall, the two did not wed. When asked the reason, Elizabeth replied that a queen could not marry her subject; it would antagonize other subjects and possibly lead to civil war.

More importantly, it would lessen her own power.

Robert Dudley was tall, dark, and handsome. In addition to being a fine athlete and a superb dancer, he loved the theater and sponsored a private company of actors.

Troublesome Mary Stuart

Actually, the main threat to Elizabeth's power was her Scottish cousin, the Catholic Mary Stuart. As the granddaughter of Henry VIII's older sister, Mary had a strong claim to the English throne, especially in Catholic eyes.

Born in 1542, Mary was named Queen of Scots as an infant. She was sent to France at the age of six to be raised in the French court. At the age of fifteen, she married the French king's son and became queen of France the following year. She returned to Scotland when her young husband died soon after.

The next few years of Mary's life read like a soap opera. In 1565, at the age of twenty-three, she married Henry Stuart, Lord Darnley, also a grandchild of Henry VIII's older sister. The marriage further strengthened Mary's claim to the English throne. Then Darnley murdered Mary's private secretary, David Riccio, who was rumored to be the father of her child. Soon after the birth of Mary's son, James Stuart, Darnley was himself found strangled to death. James Hepburn, the earl of Bothwell, was accused of the murder but was acquitted. He then kidnapped Mary, divorced his wife, and married the Queen of Scots. That was too much for the Scottish people, and the Protestant nobility, who held power in Scotland. They rose in rebellion and forced

Mary, Queen of Scots, had a creamy complexion and chestnut hair. She stood almost six feet tall.

Mary to abdicate in favor of her infant son, James VI, who would be raised a Protestant. In 1568 Mary escaped from the castle in which she had been imprisoned and sought refuge in England. (Bothwell fled to Denmark, where he died insane in prison.)

Mary's arrival presented Elizabeth with a major dilemma. Although she found her cousin's behavior appalling, she did not want to undermine another queen. So, against the advice of her privy council, she refused to send Mary back to her Scottish jail. At the same time, Elizabeth could not assist Mary in regaining her throne because that would mean going to war against Scotland. And if Mary were allowed to leave England, she probably would go to France in hopes of raising an army to invade Scotland. Elizabeth did not want French troops so close to England's borders. If Elizabeth imprisoned Mary, it would anger English Catholics. But if Elizabeth did *not* imprison Mary, it would look as if she supported her cousin's claim to the English throne.

Reluctantly, Elizabeth decided that her best course was to shift Mary from one castle to another in the northern part of England. Unfortunately, the Queen of Scots became a focus for people who wanted to overthrow Elizabeth. And Mary herself spent much of the next eighteen years conspiring with the Spanish, the French, and even the English duke of Norfolk. At last, in 1586, some of her secret letters were intercepted. In them she approved a plot to assassinate Elizabeth and take over the government with the help of Spanish soldiers and English Catholics.

Elizabeth no longer had a choice. The Queen of Scots was tried, convicted of treason, and sentenced to be executed. But killing a monarch would set a dangerous precedent. Reluctant to harm her royal cousin for fear of weakening her own power as queen,

Mary Stuart, shown here being led to her execution, always wore a crucifix as a symbol of her Roman Catholic faith.

Elizabeth at first refused to sign the death warrant. Couldn't Mary's jailer smother her instead, or put poison in her food? Finally, however, Elizabeth agreed to the execution. But after signing the death warrant, she failed to send it on to the castle where Mary was imprisoned. So Elizabeth's councilors had to take it upon themselves to forward the order.

On February 8, 1587, Mary was beheaded. As the executioner held up the wig that had come off her head, Mary's little Skye terrier crept out from beneath her petticoat and sat down next to her bloody neck.

The Spanish Armada

Mary's death was the signal for open warfare between England and Spain. The two nations had been allies for some eighty years before Elizabeth ascended the throne. Even after she became queen and rejected his offer of marriage, Philip II had supported her right to rule. Gradually, however, disputes between England and Spain had become common. They arose out of the voyages of exploration and trade that Elizabeth encouraged. Her first sea captain was John Hawkins, who made several profitable trips transporting Africans to work as slaves on Spanish plantations in the West Indies and Mexico. During his third voyage, however, the Spanish captured most of his fleet through an act of treachery. Elizabeth, who did not want war with Spain, promised Philip that English voyages to America would stop. Secretly, however, she continued to encourage them because she needed their profits to help run her government and to pay off the debts that had accumulated under her half brother, Edward VI, and her half sister, Mary Tudor.

Over the next ten years, English privateers, or pirates, carried on an undeclared war against Spain. The most outstanding of these privateers was Francis Drake. At first he raided Spanish possessions in the Caribbean. Then, in 1577, he received Elizabeth's permission to raid Spanish possessions in the Pacific. After sailing his ship

Sir Walter Raleigh, like Sir Francis Drake, was a famous privateer, and a great favorite of the queen's. There is a legend that he once spread his cloak over a puddle so that Elizabeth would not have to step in the mud.

the *Golden Hind* through the Strait of Magellan at the tip of South America, Drake plundered Spanish settlements in Chile and Peru. He then sailed across the Pacific, went around India and Africa, and returned to England in 1580. He and his sailors were the first Englishmen to go around the world! Drake brought back a fortune in silver, gold, and diamonds seized from the Spanish, and the grateful queen soon made him a knight. (With his share of the spoils, Sir Francis bought a large country estate and became a member of Parliament.)

After Drake's voyage, relations between England and Spain grew steadily worse. Then Mary Stuart was executed—and Philip II, who had grown more and more religious over the years, decided the time had come to launch a holy crusade against Protestant England. (The pope had already excommunicated Elizabeth and promised financial aid to Philip when his soldiers set foot on English soil.)

The Spanish attack was to be two-pronged. One prong would consist of the Armada, a huge fleet of ships, under the command of the duke of Medina Sidonia. The Armada would concentrate on capturing English vessels and supporting the invasion. The second prong would consist of barges carrying some eighteen thousand battle-hardened men under the command of the duke of Parma, then stationed in the Netherlands. The two prongs would rendezvous and proceed to England, where the Spanish troops would land southeast of London.

It was a grand plan. But unfortunately for Philip, it had some serious drawbacks. How were Parma and Medina Sidonia supposed to communicate with each other so they could rendezvous? While the Spanish ships were huge, they were also clumsy. Moreover, the Spanish were accustomed to a strategy of firing only one round of cannonballs before boarding an enemy vessel. They had not been trained to continue firing if the first round of shot failed to disable their opponent. In addition, Medina Sidonia, although very efficient, had no practical experience commanding ships.

The English navy was much smaller than the Armada. However, it consisted mostly of new ships that Elizabeth had ordered built. Following the advice of Sir John Hawkins and Sir Francis Drake, the builders had made these new ships extremely fast and fitted them to carry cannons rather than troops. The English strategy was to bombard and sink the enemy while staying far enough away to avoid being boarded.

The Armada, some 130 ships strong, sailed for England in May 1588. As its crescent-shaped formation approached the port of Plymouth, it was attacked by English ships. However, the English

One reason for the Armada's failure was the fact that Philip never bothered to consult with Parma and Medina Sidonia about how they would rendezvous. The king simply issued his orders and trusted in God to take care of the details.

did not do much damage, and the Armada continued on to its appointed rendezvous with Parma. He never came. Dutch Protestants had bottled up his barges in the port of Dunkirk.

On the night of August 7, as the Armada lay at anchor in the Channel, the English sent eight blazing fireships against the enemy fleet. The Spanish panicked, and their ships scattered up and down the coast. The next morning, the English moved in for the kill. The battle raged for nine hours, with the English inflicting a tremendous amount of damage. Then a strong wind came up, and the bloodied Armada managed to slip away and enter the North Sea.

The English pursued the Armada for several days but then gave up the chase. Nevertheless, the next several weeks were hell for the Spanish. Their food supplies rotted, and they were forced to throw horses and mules overboard to conserve water. Many of their ships foundered on the rocky coasts of Scotland and Ireland, where their crews drowned. Thousands of other men died of cold, disease, dysentery, and starvation. By the time the roundabout 2,500-mile journey back to Spain was over, the Armada was about half its original size.

News traveled slowly in those years. So on August 18, ten days after the Armada fled northward, the English were still unaware that they were safe from invasion. Elizabeth decided to inspect her troops, who were assembled at Tilbury, at the mouth of the Thames River. Dressed in white velvet with a silver breastplate and riding a white horse, she delivered what is probably the greatest speech of her life:

> *I have always so behaved myself that, under God, I have placed my chiefest strength and safeguard in the loyal hearts and good will of my subjects; and therefore I am come amongst you . . . being resolved, in the midst and heat of the battle, to live or die amongst you all, and to lay down for my God and for my kingdom and for my people, my honor and my blood, even in the dust. I know I have the body of a weak and feeble woman but I have*

the heart and stomach of a king, and of a king of England too and think foul scorn that Parma or Spain, or any prince of Europe should dare to invade the borders of my realm.

The Final Years

Following the defeat of the Armada, England began to expand its navy, setting the nation on its course as a future world power. Elizabethan playwrights and poets, spurred by a tremendous sense of national pride, created some of the greatest literature ever written, especially the works of William Shakespeare.

For Elizabeth, the Armada's defeat was probably the high point of her reign. For the next fifteen years, her kingdom was relatively peaceful. Her people were unified. The Church of England flourished. A rebellion led by the earl of Essex (stepson of the queen's great favorite, the earl of Leicester) was easily crushed. Although there were several years of poor harvests, as well as an outbreak of bubonic plague, the country's population increased to four or five million. A prosperous middle class of merchants and craftspeople emerged.

As time went on, though, the queen grew increasingly lonely as Leicester, Burghley, and others in her court died. Her eyesight and memory began to fail. Her temper grew worse, and she lost much of her famous energy. In January 1603 she caught a cold and could not recover. She died on March 24, aged sixty-nine and a half, older than any English monarch before her. She was succeeded on the throne by James VI of Scotland (Mary Stuart's son), who became James I of England.

Historians remember Elizabeth not because she was older than

At the time of her death, Elizabeth owned some two thousand gowns and several hundred necklaces. She is said to have worn a new gown every day.

any English monarch before her but because she was greater. The most important thing in her life was her country's welfare. She brought her people through a religious crisis without the blood-bath that afflicted much of Europe. She defeated two powerful enemies, Mary Stuart and Spain. At a time when women were not supposed to have careers, she reigned for forty-five years. She won the love of her people and the respect of Europe. Even the pope declared: "She certainly is a great queen. . . . Just look how well she governs! She is only a woman, only mistress of half an island, and yet she makes herself feared . . . by all!"

PART TWO

Elizabethan children were regarded as miniature adults. They dressed the same way as their parents, and they were not supposed to fidget, frown, fight, or talk baby talk.

in Elizabethan England

Circumfufa.fedet.digna.parente.cohors.
Talis.erat.quondam.patriarchae.menfa.Iacobi.
Menfa.fuit.Iobi.sic.cumulata.pio.
Fac.Deus.ut.multos.haec.oignat.menfa.Iofepho
Germinet.ut.Iobi.ftirps.renouata.fuit.
Fercula.praeclaro.donafti.laeta.Cobhamo
Haec.habeant.longos.gaudia.tanta.dies:
Añ.Dñi.1567.

ÆTATIS SVÆ 5 GEMELLI

ÆTA 4

Elizabethan Society

The English people were divided into several social classes. At the top, just below the royal family, was the nobility. You became a noble either by inheriting your title or, on rare occasions, by receiving it from the monarch. Next came the landed gentry, or gentlemen. Along with the nobility, they owned most of the country's land. Members of the gentry served as officers in the army and navy, and often entered such professions as law, medicine, and the church. Wealthy merchants were also considered to be gentry. Below them were the yeomen, or farmers who worked their own land. Like the upper class, yeomen could vote in parliamentary elections. Below the yeomen were craftspeople, farmers who rented their land, domestic servants and day laborers, and the unemployed poor.

Although the lines between social classes were strict, it was possible to move from one level to another. A gentleman might slide down the social scale as a result of having too many debts. A woman might marry a man with a higher social standing than her own.

In addition to social class, status in Elizabethan society depended on whether you were male or female. The man was dominant. He was looked upon as the head of the household. As one historian explains, "Husband and wife were one person—and that person was the husband. He controlled all his wife's personal property, such as clothes and jewels, as well as her land. He had the right to beat her when he chose and to oversee her religious life. He even governed her children." Nevertheless, English women had certain rights. If they became widowed, for example, they were legally recognized as independent individuals. They often took over their late husband's trade, and remarried or not as they chose.

English babies were born at home. A week or two after a child's birth it was baptized in the parish church at a ceremony sponsored by three godparents. The infant received its father's last name. First names came from various sources. There were old French names, such as William, Richard, and Henry for boys, Alice, Joan, and Jane for girls. There were saints' names, such as John and Thomas, Anne and Margaret. People were often called

Elizabethan women often bore as many as twelve children, of whom at least half were expected to die in infancy. Among the common causes of death were pneumonia and the plague.

by shortened forms of their names, such as Ned for Edward, Robin for Robert, Doll for Dorothy, and Kate for Catherine.

Marriage was a major turning point for Elizabethans because it meant that they became independent of their parents. That, in turn, meant they had to be able to support themselves. Most marriages were arranged by parents, although some Elizabethans married for love as well as for money. Brides brought with them a dowry of cash or property, which went to the groom's father. Most men married at around the age of twenty-seven, women at around the age of twenty-four. Nobles, however, usually married younger, at the ages of twenty-four and nineteen. Divorce was extremely rare.

In general, people died—as they were born—at home. Members of the upper class were buried in coffins. Their graves, which were sometimes inside the church, were marked with wood, brass, or stone signs that bore their images. Common folk were buried in woolen shrouds in the churchyard. Their graves were unmarked.

In London Town

London in Elizabethan times contained about 200,000 people. It was by far the largest city in England, as well as the third largest city in Europe (after Paris and Naples).

At that time, London was still surrounded by gated walls on three sides. Its south side was bounded by the Thames River, the city's main street. The river swarmed with traffic, from large merchant ships to small fishing boats. Rowboats called wherries served as taxis to take people either across the river or from one part of the city to another. Only one bridge spanned the Thames, Old London Bridge. It was lined with tall, narrow houses and shops. A church stood halfway across.

London itself contained more than one hundred churches, the

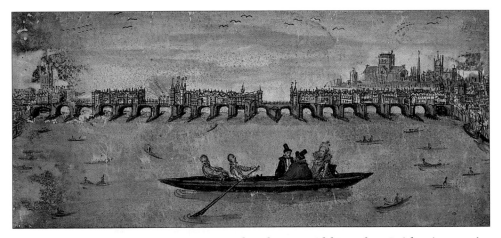

A waterman ferries passengers across the Thames. Old London Bridge is seen in the background.

largest of which was Saint Paul's Cathedral. In addition to serving as a house of worship, Saint Paul's was a social center where people met one another to gossip, show off their clothes, do business, and shop at the stands that had been set up among the tombs. The famous bookstalls in Saint Paul's churchyard were filled with "romances, jest books, histories, plays, prayer collections, and encyclopedias, all of which were eagerly purchased."

A few of London's streets were wide enough to serve as market-places. Most streets, however, were narrow and twisting. They had names, but houses were not numbered. Some streets were surfaced with cobblestones, while others were unpaved. When it rained, these turned into rivers of mud.

Most streets were also filthy, since people simply dumped their garbage outdoors. Sewage and waste from butchers' shops were thrown into the Thames. Hired scavengers collected horse droppings and carted them to dunghills on the city's outskirts. The result of this poor sanitation was an abundance of rats and other vermin, which in turn led to periodic outbreaks of disease, such as cholera, smallpox, and the plague.

London's streets were a breeding ground not only for vermin but also for criminals. Muggers lurked in the poorly lit doorways. Pickpockets and cutpurses plied their trade among the crowds. People went out at night only in groups or under the protection of hired guards. Criminals convicted for their crimes were usually hanged in public, and ordinary people (including children) were encouraged to come and watch.

Yet despite the filth and the crime, London was a lively, bustling place. It was also a wealthy place, the center of England's ever-growing overseas trade.

Housing

In the countryside, the typical upper-class manor house was built of stone or brick, often in the shape of an E (for Elizabeth). A broad stairway led from the large central hall to the upper floor. There, one usually found a gallery where children could play and ladies could stroll about on rainy days. On one side of the hall were the family bedrooms. On the other side was the service wing, which contained the kitchen, the buttery, the larder or food storage place, and the dairy. Numerous fireplaces threw off welcome heat. Walls were either paneled in wood or hung with tapestries showing biblical or legendary scenes. Floors were covered with rush mats. (Carpets served to cover furniture rather than the floor.) Elizabethan manor houses were much brighter than older houses. Windows were larger, glass was gradually replacing horn and shutters, and ceilings were lightened by plaster. There was comparatively little furniture, though, and no running water. Servants fetched water from a stream or well. Beeswax or tallow candles provided light at night.

Common folk usually lived in half-timbered cottages known as "black-and-white." These were built on a wood frame, with the beams forming one or more patterns on the outside. The spaces between the dark timbers—the "black"—were filled in with plaster—the "white." The most common roofing was thatch, which was made with reeds or straw. Thatch provided very good

Nobles' estates boasted gardens, meadows, and wooded areas. Although the houses were magnificent, they were difficult to heat.

insulation. Unfortunately, it also provided a haven for vermin and was a major fire risk. People who could afford it used clay tiles, slate, or wooden shingles instead.

Most cottages contained only two rooms. The front room was used for cooking, eating, and working. The back room was used for sleeping. If the householder was prosperous, there was a third room for preparing food. Floors were made of either wood or packed dirt. Heat came from an open hearth or, increasingly, from a fireplace with a chimney.

Town houses were similar to country cottages, except that they contained more rooms and were usually two or three stories high. The upper stories often jutted out over the street. This provided more space inside the house but also prevented sunlight from reaching the street below.

Elizabethans loved gardens, which they called "the purest of human pleasures." Rich people tried to grow different flowers for each month and to choose plants for their smell as well as their color. They delighted in fountains, mazes of hedges, and vast expanses of lawn. The gardens of country folk were more practical. In addition to flowers, they usually contained flax for making linen, herbs for cooking and medicine, and hops for making ale and beer.

Clothing, Cosmetics, and Hairstyles

People in Elizabethan England were very fashion conscious. Styles were set by the court and usually copied by everyone else.

The most popular clothing materials were linen and wool, although courtiers dressed in silk and velvet. Linen garments were left undyed, but other fabrics were dyed. Brown and gray were the cheapest colors to produce, so clothing in these colors was worn mostly by poor people. Blue dye was moderate in cost, so blue clothing was usually worn by servants. Black and bright red dyes were very expensive, so only the richest people could afford cloth in these colors. Since Elizabethans used natural dyes, all the colors soon faded.

Next to their bodies, both men and women wore a long-sleeved shirt, usually made of linen, although wealthy people preferred silk. A man's shirt reached to his thighs, while a woman's shirt fell below her knees. Most people also used the shirt as a nightgown; rich people, though, slept in special nightshirts.

On top of her shirt, an Elizabethan woman wore one, two, or three garments. The first was a long fitted dress called a kirtle. The second was a bodice and petticoat. The bodice was something like a vest and was either sleeved or sleeveless. If you had a personal maid to help you dress, it laced in back. If you were poor, the bodice laced in front. The neckline went up and down depending on the current style. The bodices of upper-class women were stiffened with whalebone, wood, or bundles of dried reeds. Since lower-class women were expected to move around while performing such tasks as "churning butter, baking bread, or chasing children," their bodices were left unstiffened. The petticoat was what we call a skirt and was worn over a series of hoops made of wire, whalebone, or wood.

The third garment, the gown, consisted of a bodice and skirt sewn together. The skirt was often left open in front to reveal the petticoat or kirtle underneath. Gowns worn by ladies of the court were richly decorated with jewels and gold and silver braid.

The style of men's garments for the lower body changed considerably during Elizabeth's reign. At first men wore trunk hose. These were onion-shaped garments that went from the waist to the top of the thighs and had vertical slashes to show a contrasting fabric underneath. Gradually the trunk hose became longer and fuller, while the vertical slashes disappeared, leaving the trunk hose a solid color. Toward the end of Elizabeth's reign, men began wearing Venetian breeches, or knee-length trousers.

The style of men's garments for the upper body remained more or less the same. The basic garment was the doublet, a short, fitted jacket with a narrow waist. In the beginning, the doublet's bottom was cut straight across. In time, however, it developed a downward V shape.

Other articles of clothing included stockings, ruffs, cassocks, and capes. Stockings were made mostly of wool or linen cloth, although, about halfway through Elizabeth's reign, some people began to wear knitted stockings. The stockings were kept in place

Only women of the highest
rank—like Catherine Parr,
who was Henry VIII's sixth
wife—wore lynx fur.

This gentleman is wearing
Venetian breeches.

with garters. Ruffs, which were made of linen, were worn around the neck. In 1565 people began using starch to stiffen their ruffs. As a result, the ruffs grew larger and larger until they needed a wire framework for support. Some ruffs eventually extended nine inches from the neck! Cassocks were long, flaring coats designed to keep their wearers warm. Fashionable men preferred circular or semicircular capes, either short or long.

Both men and women wore the same kind of blunt-toed, flat-heeled shoes, with no difference between the right and left foot. Most shoes were made of leather, but courtiers sometimes wore shoes of velvet or silk. In the earlier part of Elizabeth's reign, people slipped their feet into their shoes. In the latter part of the reign, they fastened their shoes with buckles or laces. Men wore high leather boots when riding horseback.

Both men and women wore leather belts, which were known as girdles. They were used not to hold up garments but to carry personal belongings. Men's girdles carried swords, daggers, and purses. Women's girdles carried purses, mirrors (if they were rich enough to own a mirror), and keys.

Early in Elizabeth's reign, men wore flat caps of wool, felt, or leather. Later in the reign, hats became increasingly fashionable, especially those made from beaver fur. Courtiers often trimmed their hats with a feather or a jeweled hat pin. Country folk usually wore hats made of straw. Most women covered their hair with a linen cap, on top of which they often wore a kerchief, hood, or hat.

Both men and women adorned themselves with bracelets, earrings, necklaces, and rings. Miniatures, or small portraits set in a round frame, often dangled from their necks.

Most women did not use makeup. Fashionable women, however,

The larger the ruff, the more fashionable its wearer.

imitated Elizabeth by painting their faces a pale white. Next, they applied red rouge to their cheeks and lips, and covered the paint with powder. Some women also tinted their eyelids.

In the earlier part of Elizabeth's reign, men generally wore their hair short. Later, they let it grow long. Most men sported a mustache and a beard that was usually trimmed to a point. Women usually wore their hair long but pinned it up so as to leave the forehead uncovered.

Elizabethans seldom bathed, preferring to wash themselves at a basin. (Elizabeth was considered a little peculiar because she took a bath once a month.) However, they were careful to clean their nails and comb their hair every day. Fashionable men and women masked their body odors by sprinkling themselves liberally with perfume.

Food and Drink

Few Elizabethans ate breakfast. Their real meals were dinner, which was served in the late morning around eleven o'clock or noon, and supper, which was served in the evening between six and nine. Common people ate their main meal at midday, while rich people ate theirs in the evening. Upper-class Elizabethans used knives and spoons but not forks. These had not yet been brought from Italy, where they had recently been invented. Ordinary Elizabethans used only knives; otherwise, they ate with their fingers and used cups for soups. Men placed their napkins across one shoulder; women kept theirs in their laps. It was customary to wash your hands and recite a prayer both before and after a meal.

Breakfast, when it was eaten, usually consisted of porridge or leftovers, with the occasional addition of bread and cheese. Dinner and supper featured meat, seafood, vegetables, fruit, and bread.

Elizabethans consumed a great variety of meat. There were red meats such as beef, lamb, pork, and veal. There were game meats such as deer, rabbit, and all sorts of wildfowl, ranging from sparrows and larks to partridge and pheasants. Poultry included chickens, ducks, geese, and pigeons. Seafood was also very popular, in large part because it was cheap and usually fresh. Another reason for its popularity was a rule Elizabeth issued prohibiting the eating of meat on Wednesdays, Fridays, and Saturdays, as well as on certain religious holidays such as Lent and Advent. The queen's

Dining in the Great Hall of a manor house was sometimes a casual affair.

reason for the rule was to encourage and support the English
fishing industry, as well as English sea power in general.

Most Elizabethans grew vegetables and fruits in household
gardens. The vegetables included artichokes, asparagus, beans,
cabbage, carrots, cucumbers, endive, leeks, lettuce, parsnips, peas,
radishes, spinach, and turnips. The most common domestic fruits
were apples, cherries, pears, plums, and raspberries. England also
imported oranges and lemons from Spain and Italy, but they were

too expensive for the average person. Even more expensive were potatoes from the Americas!

Few Elizabethans drank water. Poor sanitation in cities and towns, as well as natural impurities in the countryside, made it an unhealthy beverage. Instead, most people—children as well as adults—drank ale, which they made from malted barley, spices, and herbs. Ales varied in strength from light "small ales" to heavy "double-double ales" that bore such names as "Mad Dog" and "Dragon's Milk." The average person drank about one gallon of ale a day. Toward the end of Elizabeth's reign, beer—which was lighter, clearer, and cheaper than ale—became popular in the cities. Both ale and beer were not completely fermented, however. This made them much less alcoholic than they are today.

Rich Elizabethans also drank imported wines, to which they added large amounts of sugar, since they liked their wine sweet. (Some used so much sugar that their teeth often decayed and turned black.) Drinks made from homegrown fruit included cider from apples and perry from pears. Mead and metheglin were made from honey. The most popular mixed drinks were posset, a combination of ale and curdled milk that was often sugared and spiced, and syllabub, a similar drink that was soured with vinegar or cider. Only children drank milk.

Getting an Education

It is difficult to know how widespread literacy was during Elizabeth's reign. Most scholars believe that between 20 and 30 percent of men and between 5 and 10 percent of women knew how to read and write. But whatever the facts, there was no national system of public education. Schooling varied according to where you lived and how wealthy your parents were. As might be expected, literacy was highest among the upper class and in the cities.

Rich people usually hired private tutors, especially for girls. Tutors also taught specialized subjects such as French, geography, dancing, music, and fencing. Other people sent their children to "petty schools," which were generally run by the parish church. Pupils learned reading, writing, and arithmetic from a "horn book," a wooden tablet on which a sheet of text was pasted and then covered with a thin layer of horn for protection. The curriculum was strongly religious, consisting mostly of prayers and the catechism. The typical school day ran from six or seven o'clock in the morning until five o'clock in the afternoon, with a fifteen-minute break for breakfast at 9 A.M., a two-hour break for dinner at 11 A.M., and a half-hour recess at 3 P.M. There were two-week vacations at Christmas and Easter. Discipline was strict, and beating with a birch rod was common.

After petty school, many boys and a very few girls went on to grammar school, which usually lasted until the age of fourteen. Rich students paid tuition. Poor but bright students were able to obtain scholarships. Some grammar schools were full-time boarding schools, while others were day schools from which students went home for dinner. The curriculum featured Latin. This was because professionals such as doctors, lawyers, and civil servants all used a great deal of Latin in their work.

After grammar school, boys—but not girls—might attend one of England's two universities, Oxford or Cambridge. Obtaining a bachelor's degree took four years. A master's degree took an additional three years, and a doctorate in law, medicine, or divinity took another seven to twelve years. Teaching at Oxford and Cambridge was done largely by lecture. However, since both universities had their own press, more and more students began to read texts for themselves. There were also two alternative institutions of higher learning, the Inns of Court and the Inns of Chancery, where students learned law both by attending lectures and by observing proceedings in law courts and in Parliament.

Earning a Living

Most Elizabethans were farmers. Their plows were pulled by oxen rather than horses and were often owned not by individuals but by landlords or the community as a whole. Nevertheless, farmers in Elizabeth's day were becoming more productive. One reason was a system called enclosure. In the past, each farmer had cultivated scattered strips of cropland and had grazed his animals on a common pasture with the animals of other farmers. During the 1500s, farmers consolidated their fields and grazing lands and surrounded them with thick hedges. This made farming much more efficient. However, it also meant that fewer hands were needed. Tenant farmers (those who rented their land) particularly suffered as they were often thrown out of work.

Another aid to higher farm production was specialization. For some time, farmers had been market oriented. That is, they produced surpluses for sale instead of growing food just for themselves. During Elizabeth's reign, they began to increase production by concentrating on agricultural products that were best suited to their soil and climate. For example, southern England grew the most flavorful apples. The counties of Cheshire and Suffolk were noted for their cheeses, and so on.

The two leading industries of Elizabethan England were mining and textiles. Miners dug lead, tin, and especially coal. Textiles were made from wool and were the country's chief export. Their

ELIZABETHAN ENGLAND

SCOTLAND

Edinburgh

IRELAND

Dublin

IRISH SEA

York

NORTH SEA

ENGLAND

Chester

WALES

Coventry

Stratford-upon-Avon

Cambridge

Oxford

London

Tilbury

Thames River

Canterbury

Bristol

Dover

Dunkirk

Calais

Isle of Wight

Plymouth

N

ENGLISH CHANNEL

FRANCE

0   100 miles

importance is shown by the fact that, in 1588, England had almost four times as many sheep as it did people.

Throughout the land there were a large number and variety of craftspeople. There were tanners, glovers, shoemakers, tailors, butchers, bakers, carpenters, and smiths. Craftspeople not only did the work but sold it as well, usually from the front ground-floor room of their houses. You became a craftsperson through the apprenticeship system. An apprentice spent about seven years learning a trade. In exchange for his labor, he received bed and board in his master's house. Sometimes his master also taught him how to read, write, and do arithmetic.

Between the ages of about fourteen and twenty-four, a majority of Elizabethans were employed in domestic service as butlers, cooks, and maids. From there they often moved on to better positions. Men became soldiers and sailors. Women in towns sometimes worked as seamstresses, laundresses, and street vendors. An increasing number of people became merchants, especially in foreign trade. As one historian explains, "They would buy goods from several manufacturers and then arrange for their export and sale."

The growth of London's merchant class led to a mutually beneficial relationship with Elizabeth's government. On the one hand, the merchants paid high taxes that enabled the royal government to meet its bills. On the other hand, the government levied duties on foreign goods, which reduced competition for the merchants and helped them earn larger profits.

Although many merchants and others became rich, there was more unemployment under Elizabeth than there had been under previous rulers. A major reason was enclosure, which drove tenant farmers off the land and turned them into migrant laborers. In addition, soldiers wounded in the war with Spain were often unable to work.

The result was a public welfare program known as the Elizabethan Poor Laws. Financed by a poor tax that everyone had to pay, these laws concentrated on three groups of people. Children who had lost their parents were placed in orphanages and put out as apprentices when they were around seven years old. Able-bodied people unable to find jobs were sent to work-houses, where they received room and board in exchange for making salable items such as candles and rope. "Rogues, vagabonds, and sturdy beggars"—people who were able to work but didn't—were whipped the first time they were caught, burned on the right ear the second time, and put to death the third time.

Sports and Entertainments

The most popular sport was hunting. Members of the upper class favored deer hunting and often set aside forested sections of their land holdings as deer parks. Common folk were forbidden to hunt deer. Instead, they hunted such animals as badgers, foxes, and squirrels. "Coursing the hares" was especially popular. A captured hare would be released twelve yards ahead of a pack of greyhounds. The purpose was to see which dog could run the fastest.

People who preferred a less active sport than hunting went fishing, mostly for the salmon that filled many of England's rivers. Individuals angled with baited hook and line, while towns sometimes stretched nets across a stream to trap the fish.

Martial sports included archery and fencing. Upper-class men enjoyed playing tennis. In addition to horse racing, the most popular spectator sports were blood sports such as cockfighting, bearbaiting, and bullbaiting. Cockfighting involved fitting a pair of roosters with a sharp blade on each foot and having them fight to the death in a small, round arena called a "cockpit." In bearbaiting and bullbaiting, the animal was chained to a stake in the middle of a large arena. Fierce bulldogs or mastiffs were then released into the arena. The dogs would clamp their jaws on the larger animal's ears or nose, while the bear or bull would try to shake the dogs off and claw or gore them. Sometimes the bull or bear collapsed from exhaustion. At other times, it killed or disabled so many of its attackers that the rest ran away. Spectators would bet on the result.

In addition to blood sports, Elizabethans went in for team sports like hurling and football. The object in hurling was to hit a ball with a club or a stick so it would go over the opponents' goal. Some hurlers played on foot, while others were on horseback. In the countryside, where one village often carried on a traditional rivalry with a neighboring village, each side consisted of the village's entire adult male population. The playing field extended for several miles, and the opponents played on set days, such as Easter Monday, Ascension Thursday, and the feast of Corpus Christi. Football was likewise often played between villages. The players, who went on foot (hence the name "football"), tried to carry a ball across the goal. There were no rules to speak of. Whoever was holding the ball could be tackled by a member of the opposing team, and bloody noses and broken heads, legs, and backs were common.

Many groups objected to football. Puritans did so because it was often played on Sundays. Merchants and manufacturers disliked the game because the violence meant that injured players lost working time. The government objected because football took up time that it felt should be devoted to practicing archery. After all, the longbow was still England's main weapon of war, even though the gun was fast catching up.

Elizabethans also played less demanding games, such as billiards, bowls, and especially dice and cards. Dice were the favorite pastime of common folk. Everyone played cards. Many Elizabethan card

These Tudor gentlemen are playing primero, an early form of poker.

games were early versions of modern games. For example, one-and-thirty was similar to twenty-one; primero was an ancestor of poker; and noddy was an early form of cribbage.

Another popular diversion was music. The upper class favored such instruments as the lute, the viol, the recorder, and the virginal, which resembled a harpsichord. Common folk were fond of the bagpipe, the fiddle, and the pipe-and-tabor (a combination in which the left hand played a recorder while the right hand played a drum). Small orchestras performed during meals at the royal court, while many towns supported bands that played at local festivals. When Sir Francis Drake sailed around the world, he made certain there was an orchestra on board the *Golden Hind*.

Elizabethans also sang a great deal, usually in harmony rather than solo. They sang in church, at their workplaces, and in their homes. Wandering minstrels were a common sight in village squares on market day.

Dancing was almost as popular as music. The upper class preferred stately, complicated dances performed by couples. Common folk favored simple dances performed by couples in round or square sets. Summer festivals often included a form of entertainment known as morris dancing. Six or eight men would perform a lively dance to the accompaniment of bells tied around their legs just below the knee.

The Elizabethan Theater

Many scholars say the entertainment industry really started with the building of theaters during Elizabeth's reign. Before then, companies of touring actors had performed plays mostly in the courtyards of inns. The typical company consisted of seven to ten actors, all male; young boys played the women's parts. They traveled in wagons that carried their costumes, a few props, and the wooden planks that formed their portable stage. When they came to an inn, they set up their stage next to the inn's door. The audience surrounded the stage on three sides and paid a penny a person to see the show.

At that time, actors had a poor reputation. And in fact, some of that reputation was deserved. Actors often organized crooked gambling games with townspeople or picked the pockets of the audience during the play.

As Elizabeth's reign continued, many towns grew increasingly reluctant to allow traveling troupes to perform. As a result, the more honest, professional companies placed themselves under the protection of a noble. Then the Poor Laws of 1572 gave actors legal status by granting the companies licenses. Finally, in 1576, actor James Burbage built the first permanent theater, called simply The Theatre, just south of London. In the 1590s, when his land

The Globe Theatre was destroyed by the Puritans in 1644. A modern replica opened in 1997.

lease ran out, he apparently tore the building down and used its lumber to build a new theater, the Globe, on the south bank of the Thames River. The Globe became the most famous theater of the Elizabethan period and was occupied by its most famous acting company, the Lord Chamberlain's Players. Among its members was England's greatest playwright, William Shakespeare.

Going to the Globe was an exciting experience. Crowds began

William Shakespeare wrote 38 plays, as well as more than 150 poems. Many of his plots were not original but came from other sources.

gathering at noon for the two o'clock performance. (Plays were always performed during the day.) By one o'clock, some two thousand to three thousand spectators had streamed through the small entrance door and taken their places. "Groundlings" stood in the unroofed yard of the circular wood-and-plaster building. Aristocrats and wealthy merchants sat in the roofed three-story galleries that lined three sides of the yard. A few nobles sat on the rectangular stage that jutted out into the yard. The back of the stage had two doors for entrances and exits. There was also a trapdoor below the stage and a balcony with a gabled roof above the stage. Supporting the roof were two pillars painted in brilliant yellow and red.

Props were few. Most scenes depended on signs and the audience's imagination. Costumes, on the other hand, were both elaborate and gorgeous. There were also special effects, such as a rolling cannonball to imitate thunder, or blaring trumpets to signal a battle.

Audiences were not very well behaved in those days. They gossiped with their neighbors, bought hazelnuts and ale from vendors, and even threw oranges at actors whose performances did not meet with their approval.

Being an actor was hard work. You needed a powerful body (especially for fight scenes), a strong voice, and an excellent memory. You had to play a different part every day, and sometimes take on several roles in the same play. Yet despite its drawbacks, acting was a popular profession, and several leading actors became "stars" like movie or rock stars today.

PART THREE

Like archery, fencing was a sport that enabled Elizabethan men to practice for war.

Many Englishmen believed they had a God-given right to control their wives. Some used force. Writer Nicholas Breton suggested a different way for husbands to behave:

Cherish all good humors in her: let her lack no silk, crewel, thread, nor flax, to work on at her pleasure, force her to nothing, rather prettily chide her from her labor . . . [and] commend [praise] what she doeth: if she be learned and studious, persuade her to translation, it will keep her from idleness, and it is a cunning kind task; if she be unlearned, commend her to housewifery, and make much of her carefulness, and bid her servants take example at their mistress. . . . At table be merry to her, abroad be kind to her, always be loving to her, and never be bitter to her, for patient Griselda is dead long ago, and women are flesh and blood.

The printing press arrived in England from Germany in 1476. Its impact was tremendous, and hundreds of books soon made their appearance. Sir Francis Bacon (1561–1626), a philosopher, statesman, and scientist, wrote the following appreciation of the purposes and pleasures of reading:

Read not to contradict and confute [prove wrong]; nor to believe and take for granted; nor to find talk and discourse; but to weigh and consider. Some books are to be tasted, others to be swallowed, and some few to be chewed and digested: that is, some books are to be read only in parts; others to be read, but not curiously; and some few to be read wholly, and with diligence and attention. Some books also may be read by deputy, and extracts made of them by others; but that would be only in the less important arguments and the meaner sort of books; else distilled books are like common distilled waters, flashy things. Reading maketh a full man; conference a ready man; and writing an exact man. And therefore, if a man write little, he had need have a great memory; if he confer little, he had need have a present wit; and if he read little, he had need have much cunning, to seem to know that he doth not. Histories make men wise; poets, witty; the mathematics, subtle; natural philosophy, deep; moral [philosophy], grave; logic and rhetoric, able to contend [argue].

The rose tree
against which
this young man
is leaning
symbolizes his
feelings of love.

In addition to books, Elizabethans were very fond of poems, which dealt mostly with love. The sonnet, a fourteen-line poem with a set rhythm and rhyme pattern, was a popular poetic form. Shakespeare's Sonnet Number Eighteen is an example:

Shall I compare thee to a summer's day?
Thou art more lovely and more temperate:
Rough winds do shake the darling buds of May,
And summer's lease hath all too short a date:
Sometime too hot the eye of heaven shines,
And often is his gold complexion dimm'd;
And every fair from fair sometime declines,
By chance, or nature's changing course, untrimm'd;
But thy eternal summer shall not fade,
Nor lose possession of that fair thou ow'st;
Nor shall Death brag thou wand'rest in his shade,
When in eternal lines to time thou grow'st;
So long as men can breathe, or eyes can see,
So long lives this, and this gives life to thee.

Another form of poetry popular during the Elizabethan Age was the ballad. It dealt with a dramatic event and was composed to be sung. During the 1580s, a series of witchcraft trials took place in England. Many ballads describing these trials were printed and sold to the public. They were something like the *National Enquirer* and tabloid newspapers today. In the example that follows, three "witches," betrayed by their own children, meet their fate:

*A New Ballad of the Life and Deaths of Three
Witches Arraigned and Executed at Chelmsford
5 July 1589*

*List Christians all unto my Song
'Twill move your Hearts to Grace.
That Dreadful Witchcraft hath been done,
Of late about this place;
But Three that cried the Devil's Name
With those who did them follow.
Now to Justice are brought home
To swing upon our Gallow. . . .*

*As to the Story now to tell
The Truth I will Declare,
It was the Witches Children small
That they did not Beware;
For God into these infants' Hearts
Did pour the Light of Reason,
And all against their Mothers spoke
Of Witchcraft and of Treason.*

*So listen Christians to my Song
The Hangman's swung his rope,
And on these Gallows hath been done
An end to Satan's Hope;
Give the News from Chelmsford Town
To all the world be spread,
A crew of Evil Witches have gone Down
Hang'd by the neck, all three are Dead.*

The chief holiday of the year for Elizabethans (except Puritans) was Christmas. The following description of the holiday celebration was written by Nicholas Breton:

> It is now Christmas, and not a cup of drink must pass without a carol; the beasts, fowl, and fish come to general execution; and the corn is ground to dust for the bakehouse, and the pastry. Cards and dice purge many a purse. . . . Now "Good cheer" and "Welcome," and "God

Musicians "make their instruments speak out" during a holiday celebration in an upper-class household.

*be with you," and "I thank you," and "Against the new
year," provide for the presents. . . . Piping and dancing
puts away much melancholy. Stolen venison is sweet, and
a fat coney [rabbit] is worth money. Pit-falls are now set
for small birds, and a woodcock hangs himself in a gin [a
trap for game]. A good fire heats all the house, and a full
alms-basket makes the beggars prayers. The masquers and
mummers [actors] make the merry sport. . . . Swearers
and swaggerers are sent away to the ale-house. . . .
Musicians now make their instruments speak out, and a
good song is worth the hearing. In sum, it is a holy time,
a duty in Christians for the remembrance of Christ, and
custom among friends for the maintenance of good
fellowship. In brief, I thus conclude of it: I hold it a
memory of the Heaven's love and the world's peace, the
mirth of the honest, and the meeting of the friendly.*

Puritans not only disapproved of celebrating Christmas. They
also disapproved of dancing, cardplaying, and sports of any kind.
A good Puritan woman spent her time like Lady Margaret Hoby:

*In the morning after private prayers and order taken for
dinner I wrote some notes in my Testament till 10 o'clock;
then I went to walk and, after I returned home, I prayed*

privately, read a chapter of the Bible, and wrought [embroidered] till dinner time. After, I walked awhile with Mr. Rhodes [her chaplain] and then I wrought and did some good things about the house till 4. Then I wrote out the sermon into my book preached the day before and, when I had again gone about in the house and given order for supper and other things, I returned to examination and prayer. Then I walked till supper time and, after catechising [studying scripture], meditated awhile of that I had heard, with mourning to God for pardon both of my omission and commission wherein I found myself guilty, I went to bed.

Even before the invention of the automobile, London suffered from traffic problems. The following complaint was written in the 1580s by chronicler John Stow:

The number of cars, drays [heavy carts], carts and coaches more than hath been accustomed, the streets and lanes being straitened [narrow], must needs be dangerous, as daily experience proveth. The coachman rides behind the horse tails, lasheth them and looketh not behind him; the drayman sitteth and sleepeth on his dray and letteth his horse lead him home. I know that by the good laws and customs of this city, shod carts are forbidden to enter the same except upon reasonable causes, as service of the prince or suchlike . . . ; also that the forehorse of every carriage should be led by hand—but these good orders are not observed. Now of late years the use of coaches . . . is

Outside London in Elizabeth's day, when roads were rutted and overgrown, coaches were rarely used and most people traveled by foot.

taken up and made so common [that] . . . difference of persons [is no longer] observed; for the world runs on wheels with many whose parents were glad to go on foot.

Elizabethans who made colonial voyages to North America found a people whose way of life differed greatly from their own. Thomas Hariot, who explored what is now Virginia, wrote the following description of "Red Indians" in 1588:

They are a people clothed with loose mantles made of deer skins, and aprons of the same round about their middles; all else naked. . . . [They have] no edge tools or weapons of iron or steel to offend us withall, neither know they how to make any: those weapons that they have, are only bows made of witch-hazel, and arrows of reeds, flat edged truncheons [short clubs] also of wood about a yard long, neither have they anything to defend themselves but targets [shields] made of barks, and some armours made of sticks wickered together with thread.

Their towns are but small, and near the sea coast but few, some containing but 10 or 12 houses, some 20, the greatest that we have seen have been but of 30 houses: if they be walled it is only done with barks of trees made fast to stakes, or else with poles only fixed upright and close one by another. . . .

In respect of us they are a people poor, and for want of skill and judgement in the knowledge and use of our things, do esteem our trifles before things of greater value; notwithstanding . . . they seem very ingenious; for although they have no such tools, nor any such crafts, sciences and arts as we, yet in those things they do [have], they show excellency of wit. . . . Whereby may be hoped, if means of good government be used, that they may in short time be brought to civility, and the embracing of true religion.

Some religion they have already, which although it be far from the truth, yet being as it is, there is hope it may be the easier and sooner reformed.

Among the products that Elizabethans brought back from North America was tobacco. At first—as the following account explains—it was believed to have various medicinal qualities. However, its dangerous effects soon appeared. Thomas Hariot, quoted in the previous reading, is believed to have been the first European to die from cancer caused by smoking:

It is usually larger than our comfrey [a medicinal herb], though found flourishing in the same well-watered spots

According to this French manuscript written during Elizabeth's reign, the Indians used tobacco for food as well as medical purposes.

of rich earth, exposed to the sun. It has very wide leaves, of oblong shape, hairy quality, wider, rounder, larger than those of comfrey. . . . The stalk grows three cubits high in France, Belgium and England. . . . It bears flower calyxes in August of a pale, somewhat reddish green. . . . For you will observe shipmasters [sailors] and all others who come back from out there [America] using little funnels, made of palm leaves or straw, in the extreme end of which they stuff [crumbled dried leaves] of this plant. This they light, and opening their mouths as much as they can, they suck in the smoke with their breath. By this they say their hunger and thirst are allayed [eased], their strength restored, and their spirits refreshed. . . . Our age has discovered nothing from the New World which will be numbered among the remedies more valuable and efficacious [effective] than this plant for sores, wounds, affections of the throat and chest, and the fever of the plague.

Glossary

bowls: A game played on a level lawn in which the players try to roll irregularly shaped wooden balls as close as possible to a target without hitting it.

chide: To scold mildly.

cubit: A distance of seventeen to twenty-two inches; a cubit was originally the distance from the elbow to the tip of the middle finger.

dowry: The money or property that a bride brings to a marriage.

dunghill: A pile of manure.

hierarchy: Order of authority; a series of ranks or grades with each level under the one above.

litter: An enclosed coach mounted on two wooden poles, used to carry a single passenger.

manor: A large estate.

mastiff: A large, powerful dog.

pageant: A costume play, usually about historical or legendary events.

parish: A church district.

Parliament: The legislative body of English government.

patient Griselda: The long-suffering heroine of a medieval story; Griselda's husband inflicts one trial after another on her to test her devotion, and she bears them all very patiently.

precedent: An action or decision that may serve as an example to be followed in the future.

privy: Private.

radical: Favoring extreme changes or reforms.

recorder: An old-style flute.

rhetoric: The effective use of speech and writing.

shroud: A burial wrap.

vermin: Small animals or insects, such as rats or cockroaches, that carry disease.

For Further Reading

Ashby, Ruth. *Elizabethan England*. New York: Marshall Cavendish, 1999.

Lace, William W. *Elizabethan England*. San Diego: Lucent Books, 1995.

Marrin, Albert. *The Sea King: Sir Francis Drake and His Times*. New York: Atheneum Books for Young Readers, 1995.

Stanley, Diane, and Peter Vennema. *Good Queen Bess*. New York: Four Winds Press, 1990.

White-Thompson, Stephen. *Elizabeth I and Tudor England*. New York: The Bookwright Press, 1985.

Zamoyska, Betka. *Queen Elizabeth I*. New York: McGraw Hill, 1981.

ON-LINE INFORMATION*

http://www.royal.gov.uk/history/
> An interesting site that contains information on the kings and queens of England since 802.

http://www.britainexpress.com/History/Tudor_index.htm
> This site describes the people and events of Tudor England and has links to other aspects of English history and culture.

*Websites change from time to time. For additional on-line information, check with the media specialist at your local library.

Bibliography

Ashby, Ruth. *Elizabethan England*. New York: Marshall Cavendish, 1999.

Dodd, A. H. *Life in Elizabethan England*. Ruthin, North Wales: John Jones Publishing, Ltd., 1998.

Erickson, Carolly. *The First Elizabeth*. New York: Summit Books, 1983.

Evans, G. Blakemore, ed. *The Riverside Shakespeare*. Boston: Houghton Mifflin Company, 1974.

Gross, Susan Hill, and Marjorie Wall Bingham. *Women in Medieval/ Renaissance Europe*. St. Louis Park, MN: Glenhurst Publications, 1983.

Hogrefe, Pearl. *Women of Action in Tudor England*. Ames, IA: Iowa State University Press, 1977.

Hurstfield, Joel, and Alan G. R. Smith. *Elizabethan People: State and Society*. New York: St. Martin's Press, 1972.

Lace, William W. *Elizabethan England*. San Diego: Lucent Books, 1995.

Singman, Jeffrey L. *Daily Life in Elizabethan England*. Westport, CT: Greenwood Press, 1995.

Smith, Lacey Baldwin. *The Horizon Book of the Elizabethan World*. New York: The American Heritage Publishing Co., 1967.

Thomas, Jane Resh. *Behind the Mask: The Life of Queen Elizabeth I*. New York: Clarion Books, 1998.

Notes

A New Age

Page 4 "a passionate loyalty": Lace, *Elizabethan England*, p. 112.

Part One: "She Certainly Is a Great Queen"

Page 8 "head of the English Church": Thomas, *Behind the Mask*, p. 8.

Page 10 "ancient and sad": Thomas, *Behind the Mask*, p. 29.

Page 10 "a virtuous maid": Thomas, *Behind the Mask*, p. 44.

Page 10 "Already she understood": Thomas, *Behind the Mask*, p. 44.

Page 11 "back to the true Church": Thomas, *Behind the Mask*, p. 51.

Page 18 "Everywhere she went": Thomas, *Behind the Mask*, p. 110.

Page 21 "religious conformity": Singman, *Daily Life in Elizabethan England*, p. 25.

Page 22 "Behold . . . the Pledge": Thomas, *Behind the Mask*, p. 95.

Page 32 "I have always so behaved": Smith, *The Horizon Book of the Elizabethan World*, pp. 289–290.

Page 35 "She certainly is": Hogrefe, *Women of Action in Tudor England*, p. 233.

Part Two: Everyday Life in Elizabethan England

Page 38 "Husband and wife": Ashby, *Elizabethan England*, p. 58.

Page 42 "romances, jest books": Smith, *The Horizon Book of the Elizabethan World*, p. 129.

Page 45 "the purest": Smith, *The Horizon Book of the Elizabethan World*, p. 143.

Page 47 "churning butter": Singman, *Daily Life in Elizabethan England*, p. 98.

Page 58 "They would buy goods": Lace, *Elizabethan England*, p. 25.

Part Three: The Elizabethans in Their Own Words

Page 70 "Cherish all good humors": Singman, *Daily Life in Elizabethan England*, p. 18.

Page 71 "Read not to contradict": Hurstfield and Smith, *Elizabethan People: State and Society*, p. 87.

Page 72 "Shall I compare thee": Evans, *The Riverside Shakespeare*, p. 1752.

Page 74 "List Christians all": Gross and Bingham, *Women in Medieval/Renaissance Europe*, p. 129.

Page 75 "It is now Christmas": Smith, *The Horizon Book of the Elizabethan World*, p. 140.

Page 76 "In the morning": Hurstfield and Smith, *Elizabethan People: State and Society*, p. 129.

Page 77 "The number of cars": Smith, *The Horizon Book of the Elizabethan World*, p. 137.

Page 79 "They are a people": Hurtsfield and Smith, *Elizabethan People: State and Society*, pp. 41–42.

Page 80 "It is usually larger": Hurstfield and Smith, *Elizabethan People: State and Society*, pp. 100–101.

Index

Page numbers for illustrations are in **boldface**

Photo Credits